WILD CATS

Jaguars

Anne Welsbacher

ABDO Publishing Company

visit us at
www.abdopub.com

Published by Abdo Publishing Company 4940 Viking Drive, Edina, Minnesota 55435. Copyright © 2000 by Abdo Consulting Group, Inc. International copyrights reserved in all countries. No part of this book may be reproduced in any form without written permission from the publisher.

Published 2000
Printed in the United States of America
Second Printing 2002

Photo credits: Peter Arnold, Inc.

Edited by Lori Kinstad Pupeza
Contributing editor Morgan Hughes

Library of Congress Cataloging-in-Publication Data

Welsbacher, Anne, 1955-
    Jaguars / Anne Welsbacher.
    p. cm. -- (Wild cats)
    Includes index.
    Summary: Describes the physical characteristics, habitat, and behavior of jaguars, large wild cats that live in Mexico, Central and South America.
    ISBN 1-57765-090-5
    1. Jaguar--Juvenile literature. [1. Jaguar.] I. Title. II. Series: Welsbacher, Anne, 1955- Wild cats.
    QL737.C23W4465 2000
    599.75'5--dc21   98-6649
                                                        CIP
                                                        AC

Contents

Wild Cats around the World

*T*he jaguar is one kind of wild cat. Jaguars live in South America, Central America, and Mexico. Once they lived in the southwestern United States, too. Other big cats live in Africa and Asia.

Jaguars have spots that help them blend in with the land around them. Leopards have spots, too, and look like jaguars. Other wild cats have stripes or no marks at all.

All big cats are good hunters. They have sharp claws and teeth. They chase animals, catch them, and eat them.

Each kind of wild cat is good at something. Jaguars are good swimmers. Unlike most big cats, they love to be in the water!

Jaguars also are very strong. They have thick muscles. They can carry heavy weight for long distances.

Central America

South America

An alert jaguar.

Big Cat, Little Cat

If you have a house cat, you already know many things about wild cats. That is because small cats and big cats are alike in many ways.

Big cats have sharp claws, just like house cats. Both big and little cats can see at night—better than you can!

Both big and little cats are good hunters. And many kinds of cats like to climb trees.

Most cats are very graceful. That means they can keep their balance standing on branches or jumping down from high places. But jaguars are not as graceful as most cats.

House cats purr. Many big cats roar. Jaguars don't roar, but they make loud snarls and grunts.

House cats lie with their tails curled up close. Most big cats stretch their tails out long.

House cats crouch over their food to eat. Wild cats often lie down to eat.

Jaguars can see very well at night.

A Closer Look

Jaguars have spots all over their bodies. The spots look like circles. Many of the circles have a dot in the middle.

Most jaguars are tan, with black spots. Some jaguars are black. But you can still see the darker spots against their black coats. Even the rare albino (all-white) jaguar has spots, but they're hard to see.

Jaguars are very **muscular**. They have thick necks and short, strong legs. They have wide heads and big chests. They have strong jaws that can bite into food!

Leopards also have spots, and it can be hard to tell them apart from jaguars. But the two kinds of cats are different in many ways.

Leopard spots do not have dots in the middle. Jaguars are bigger and stronger. One jaguar weighs as much as two or more leopards!

Jaguars have spots all over their bodies.

The Jaguar at Home

The land and weather where an animal lives is called its **habitat**. Jaguars like habitats that are dark and wet. They like to be near rivers or swamps.

Jaguars often live in jungles and thick forests. Black jaguars like jungles because their dark fur blends with the jungle shadows. But jaguars also live in mountains and deserts.

Jaguars cool off by resting in streams. They love the water more than any other cat!

A jaguar cub drinks water while its mother watches for predators.

A Heavyweight Champion

Jaguars are very strong. A jaguar can pull a dead animal a long distance, even an animal that weighs as much as six or more jaguars! Jaguars can carry heavy animals while swimming, too.

Jaguars are good swimmers. They like to hide near water. They like to swim in rivers looking for food to eat.

Jaguars are good at hiding. Even if you were near a jaguar, you probably would never see it. Its spots keep it well hidden in dark forests.

Though they are very strong, jaguars rarely attack people. In fact, a long time ago, people in South America raised jaguars as pets.

Jaguars can run fast when needed. But they like to walk. They also like to sleep and take many naps during the day!

Jaguars are good swimmers and like to hunt for fish.

The Predator's Prey

Jaguars are **carnivores**. They are also **predators**. They eat other animals, called **prey**.

Jaguars eat animals on land and in water. They hunt, climb trees, and fish for food.

Jaguars eat capybara, animals that look like huge rats. They also eat wild pigs, monkeys, deer, and sloths.

Jaguars also eat turkeys, turtles, armadillos, and even crocodiles! Their strong jaws can crush tough skins or shells. The jaguar is the only cat that battles crocodiles.

Jaguars hunt by crouching very low. A jaguar hunting looks like a snake slithering along the ground! It kills by hitting an animal's head with its paw or by biting right through the animal's skull.

The jaguar hunts by standing quietly in the water. It waits for a fish to swim past it. Then it hits the fish with its paw, grabs it with its claws, and eats it!

Jaguars hunt by crouching very low.

Cat to Cat

*J*aguars, like many cats, are **secretive**. They like to stay hidden and private.

They like to be on their own. They travel alone for hundreds of miles, looking for food to eat and water to drink. They hunt alone, too.

Most male jaguars have their own **territories**. A territory is the section of land that a certain animal lives in and calls its own.

Male and female jaguars live together when it is time to **mate**. But when mating is done, they go off on their own again.

16

Two jaguars fighting for territory.

Cat Families

The female jaguar raises her babies, called cubs, alone. In southern **habitats**, cubs are born any time of year. In colder northern habitats, they are born in the summer.

The jaguar gives birth to cubs near rocks, trees, or bushes. Here they are hidden from other **predators**. The mother jaguar has from two to four cubs.

The cubs weigh up to two pounds (one kg) or less at birth. This is about the weight of a small melon.

Opposite page: A mother jaguar licking her cub.

Growing Up

*A*t first, the cubs **nurse** their mother. Later, she brings meat to them from her hunting trips.

When they are about six weeks old, the cubs join their mother on her hunting trips. They learn to hunt by watching her.

They practice hunting for two years. Then they are old enough to be on their own. When they are three years old, the young jaguars can have their own cubs. When they are four, they are adult jaguars.

Today, most jaguars live in zoos or special parks, called **preserves**, where they are safe from hunters. In 1984, the world's first park just for jaguars opened in Belize, a country in Central America.

Jaguars can live to be 20 years old in zoos or parks.

A mother jaguar playing with her cub.

Glossary

Carnivore—an animal that eats meat.

Habitat—the area and climate that an animal lives in.

Mate—to join in a pair in order to produce young.

Muscular—having muscles, strength.

Nurse—baby jaguars getting milk from their mother.

Predator—an animal that eats other animals.

Preserve—a special park for animals that are in danger of dying out; in the park, the animals are safe from hunters and other threats to their lives.

Prey—an animal that is eaten by other animals.

Secretive—hidden and alone, staying away from others.

Territory—an area or place where certain animals live; if others enter this area, the animal might fight or scare them off.

Internet Sites

Tiger Information Center
http://www.5tigers.org/
The Tiger Information Center is dedicated to providing information to help preserve the remaining five subspecies of tigers. This is a great site, with many links, sound, and animation.

The Lion Research Center
http://www.lionresearch.org/
Everything you want to know about lions is here. Lion research and conservation in Africa, information on lion behavior, and updates from researchers in the Serengeti about specific lion prides.

The Cheetah Spot
http://ThingsWild.com/cheetah2.html
This is a cool spot with sound and animation. Lots of fun information.

Amur Leopard
http://www.scz.org/asian/amurl1.html
This site links you to some great zoo spots. Very informative.

These sites are subject to change. Go to your favorite search engine and type in "cats" for more sites.

PASS IT ON

Tell Others What You Like About Animals!

To educate readers around the country, pass on interesting tips about animals, maybe a fun story about your animal or pet, and little-known facts about animals. We want to hear from you!

To get posted on the ABDO Publishing Company Web site, email us at "animals@abdopub.com" Visit us at www.abdopub.com

Index